P9-BJQ-101

Rain Forest

The Latest Information and Hands-on Activities to Explore Animals, Plants, and Geography

by Robin Bernard

SCHOLASTIC
PROFESSIONAL BOOKS

NEW YORK ◆ TORONTO ◆ LONDON ◆ AUCKLAND ◆ SYDNEY

DEDICATION

To Tess for all the paints and brushes; to Irving for the chariot mornings; and as always, to Jer, for the dinosaur's lunch.

ACKNOWLEDGMENTS

My thanks to Liza Charlesworth, whose gentle editorial skills continue to delight and amaze me; and to Terry Cooper, whose encouragement led me to discover places beyond East Africa.

Teachers may photocopy the designated reproducible pages for classroom use. No other part of this publication may be reproduced in whole or in part, or stored in a retrieval system, or transmitted in any form or by any means electronic, mechanical, photocopying, recording, or otherwise, without written permission of the publisher. For information regarding permission, write to Scholastic Inc., 555 Broadway, New York, NY 10012.

Cover design by Jaime Lucero and Vincent Ceci.

Text and interior design by Ellen Matlach Hassell
for Boultinghouse & Boultinghouse, Inc.

Interior illustration by Robin Bernard, Delana Bettoli, and Manuel Rivera.

PHOTO CREDITS Cover: Tree ferns: ©1982 by Lawrence E. Naylor; Macaw: ©1996 by Frank Anthony Cara; Frog: © by Schafer & Hill/Peter Arnold, Inc.; Plant: ©1993 by Kevin Schafer. **Interior:** ©1995 PhotoDisc, Inc. All rights reserved. Images ©1995 PhotoLink.

ISBN 0-590-59919-4

Copyright © 1996 by Robin Bernard. All rights reserved.

Printed in the U.S.A.

CONTENTS

People and Products

Disappearing Act

Merry Moka (CELEBRATION)

LAUNCHING A RAIN FOREST UNIT

Welcome to the jungle! The information and activities in this book are designed to help make the study of rain forests an exciting exploration for you and your students. Before starting the journey, here are some hints and ideas to help you get the most out of your rain forest unit.

Blue and yellow macaw

🍃 **ENLIST STUDENTS' HELP IN BUILDING THE UNIT.** A KWL chart (page 11) will help you discover what students want to know about rain forests. For instance, they may be far more curious about why certain animals are brightly colored than numbers of species. Use their questions to create a focus for the unit. Students can revisit the KWL chart during the course of the unit as they find the answers to many of their questions and add them to the "Learned" column.

🍃 **CREATE A JUNGLE ATMOSPHERE.** Building a Canopy Corner (page 12) at the beginning of the unit will get students started on their learning adventure. A discovery table beneath paper leaves and vines makes a great place to display rain forest books, posters, and student artwork. It won't take long for the jungle to take over as trailing vines, tribal masks, and bright-billed toucans spill onto the walls and windows of the whole room. Students can choose a name for their classroom jungle.

🍃 **TAKE A TOUR.** Browse through this book to find the activities that are most appropriate for your students and include the material you want to teach. Will you use every one? Unlikely—but you'll find many projects that will, like the rain forest itself, keep branching out as they encourage growing curiosity. Change the activities, create new ways of using them, and adapt them to suit the needs of your class.

🍃 **JOURNEY THROUGH THE JUNGLE WITH BOOKS.** How can students experience the rain forest without bugs, poisonous snakes, and steamy weather? Books can guide students through dense jungles without as much as a mosquito bite. Enrich their travels by putting together a collection of fiction and non-fiction rain forest books (see Book Breaks on page 78 for suggestions). You can set aside quiet time for reading as well as read-alouds.

🍃 **PUT IT ALL TOGETHER.** The plants and animals of the rain forest come in an amazing array of shapes and colors. Celebrate students' work on bulletin boards, hall displays, and posters. Invite other classes to visit the Canopy Corner to explore the discovery table and see the masks, books, puppets, plants, and paintings your class has collected and created.

LIVING LAYERS

Peruvian Amazon iguana

Tall Green Tales

Magenta mushrooms? Blue frogs? Just imagine how we might have responded to the accounts of early rain forest explorers. Think how their tales would have seemed even more fantastic as they told us of other wonders they discovered in the steamy green jungle: fruit-eating fish, fish-eating bats, bird-eating spiders, insect-eating plants, and flying snakes! Would we have believed them?

Diverse and Complex Environments

Tropical rain forests astonish us with their beauty and diversity of life. Although they cover less than 6 percent of Earth's surface, *more than half* the world's plant and animal species are found in them. Scientists have described the riches of these ecosystems as "nature's combination of Fort Knox and the Louvre." Rain forests are also the source of many of our favorite foods and a quarter of our pharmaceuticals—including treatments for leukemia, Hodgkin's disease, and malaria. But even if we could produce all our medicines from chemicals; even if we could manage without chocolate, cashews, and coffee; even if the survival of known and as yet undiscovered species wasn't of great importance—the benefits of rain forests would still be monumental. By recycling and filtering water, cleansing the air, and regulating global temperature, rain forests sustain the health of our planet.

Hot and Humid

There are rain forests in some mountainous regions as well as a few temperate rain forests like the one in the northwestern United States. But about 70 percent of rain forests are the lowland tropical ones, the kind we think of when we hear the word *jungle*. And the word *rain* can't be taken lightly; a forest doesn't qualify as a rain forest unless it receives more than 80 inches of precipitation a year. Even that, however, is a low-end amount, since 150 inches is common and some areas exceed 400 inches!

Spanning the equator, tropical rain forests receive sunlight for 12 hours each day, resulting in generally high temperatures. Humidity is another major characteristic, produced by the combination of heat and heavy rainfall. Uncomfortable conditions? Not for trees, shrubs, and ferns. The climate couldn't be better to support an abundance of plant life, which in turn provides food and shelter for an astounding number of animal species.

FOREST FACT

The Hawaiian rain forest on the island of Kauai gets about 460 inches of rain a year.

Green, Top to Bottom

Only about 5,000 kinds of plants, or species, have been studied so far, but botanists think there are at least 250,000. In two and a half acres of midwestern temperate forest, there are usually seven or eight kinds of trees; in the same-size patch of rain forest, there may be more than three hundred kinds.

Because of the year-round growing seasons, rain forest animals and plants interact more than any others, and they have had millions of years to develop survival strategies as predator or prey, competitors or symbiotic partners. Plants need to protect themselves against predatory behavior, but at the same time they need to reproduce. Flowering plants use color, scent, and specific structures to attract bats, birds, and insects as pollen carriers. Once a flower has been fertilized, it develops fruit containing the seeds of the next generation. The fruits tend to be sweet, juicy, and brightly colored, which attract other animals that eat the flesh and spread the seeds.

FOREST FACT

Ninety percent of all vine species are found in tropical rain forests.

The layers of a tropical rain forest provide a home to about half the world's species of plants and animals. Because each layer has a somewhat different environment, many of the plants, and consequently the animal residents, are unique to a particular layer. Although all the layers have things in common, each has specific needs and serves different purposes. Rain forest plants also have a variety of functions and tend to grow in the layer that gives them the amount of sunlight they need. Each layer receives less sunlight than the one above it, with only a small fraction of sunshine reaching the forest floor.

FOREST FACT

More than 20,000 different kinds of plants grow in Ecuador's rain forest.

Squirrel monkey

The Layers of a Rain Forest

EMERGENT LAYER

Thrusting their leafy heads above the canopy platform, the emergent trees are 130 to 180 feet tall. These giant trees are thinly dispersed (only one or two in every couple of acres) and are drenched in open sunlight. They generally have small pointy leaves, long straight trunks with few branches, and very shallow root systems. To support their mass, many species grow "buttresses"—broad woody roots that spread horizontally just under the forest floor. When these giants, weakened by damage or old age, fall, they create a wide clearing and allow sunlight to reach the smaller trees, which eventually replace them.

Scientists are coming up with new techniques to study this once inaccessible part of the jungle, including an inflatable "sky-raft" that literally sits on top of the rain forest. The more scientists look, the more they find. For instance, biologists increased a previous estimate of 2 million insect species to 30 million!

CANOPY

The limbs and leaves of the tall slender trees form a dense platform of vegetation 60 to 130 feet off the ground. This is the canopy—the layer supporting the majority of rain forest animals. Insects hum and nibble, reptiles slither along limbs, monkeys chatter as they swing between branches, and jewel-colored birds dart among leaves. The canopy offers such an abundance of shelter and food that many animals never need to descend.

Apes in the understory

8

Catching most of the sunshine, the canopy allows only a tiny amount of light to reach the ground. The leaves on their knobby crowns also absorb the first impact of rain, but they have pointed shapes that form little spouts or "drip tips" that allow water to run off. This keeps the leaf surfaces dry and discourages mold and mildew.

FOREST FACT

Having short wings makes it easier for birds to fly among the dense foliage.

UNDERSTORY

The understory rises to about 60 feet and consists of the trunks of canopy trees, shrubs, plants, and smaller trees. Some of the young saplings are slow growing, waiting for a giant to come crashing down and give them space and sunlight. Many remain in the shadows, their crowns growing long and pointed as they seek light.

While some plants grow huge leaves—up to 20 feet—to absorb as much light as possible, many have adapted to growing in shade and don't need much light for photosynthesis. Others, like the woody vines called lianas, attach themselves to young trees. As the saplings grow, the vines get a free ride toward the light, and once reaching the canopy may spread out among many trees.

FOREST FACT

Rain forest vines can be 300 feet long.

THE FOREST FLOOR

The image we often see in movies of people hacking through jungles with machetes is necessary only near a river or some other clearing where sunlight reaches the floor. Most of the rain forest's ground level is in deep shade, and plant life is quite sparse.

Soil quality on the rain forest floor is very poor compared to temperate forests. A lot of "litter" falls to the ground (about 5 tons per acre every year!) in the form of leaves, limbs and trunks, and the remains of dead animals. The debris breaks down very quickly because of the high temperature, humidity, and the activity of termites, earthworms, and fungi. The organic matter, recycled into nutrients, tends to stay on the surface where it's quickly absorbed by the trees' shallow roots.

Orchids

Epiphytes— High-Living Guests

There are about 30,000 kinds of plants called epiphytes, that never touch the ground. In a development rarely found outside a rain forest, mosses, ferns, bromeliads, orchids, and even small trees attach their roots to large "host" trees in order to gain access to more light and wind. Since they can't soak up water from the ground, their aerial roots absorb moisture and nutrients from the air. Many store water in their stems, or between overlapped leaves, and a variety of arboreal animals use them as convenient oases.

Epiphytes differ from parasitic plants in that they don't drain nourishment from their hosts. On the contrary, by trapping dust and decaying leaves, they create a soil mulch so rich in nutrients that host trees often sprout roots from their branches in order to tap into the epiphytes' pantry.

Orchids

ACTIVITIES

Parrot Talk KWL (LANGUAGE ARTS)

MATERIALS reproducible page 18 ◆ paper ◆ colored markers
◆ crayons ◆ tape or stapler

A KWL classroom chart helps students to keep track of what they
Know about tropical rain forests, what they **W**ant to find out, and
what they've **L**earned.

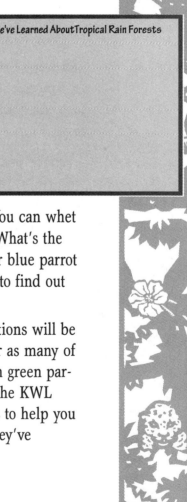

Parrot Pattern

DIRECTIONS

1. Make copies of the parrot pattern on page 18. Have students
   color some red, some blue, and some green. All can have yellow
   beaks.

2. Divide a section of wall or a bulletin board into three parts, with the third section
   twice the size of the first two. Label the first *What We Know About Tropical Rain
   Forests;* the second *What We Want to Find Out,* and the third *What We've
   Learned About Tropical Rain Forests.*

3. Challenge students to write
   facts they already know about
   the rain forest, such as "Many
   monkeys live there" or "Rain
   forests are hot and wet," on
   red parrot shapes. Collect the
   red parrots, sort out the dupli-
   cate facts, and attach them in
   the **K**now section.

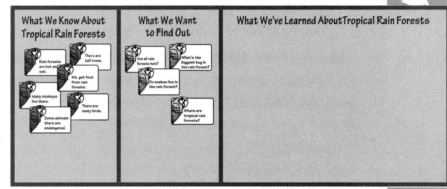

4. Then ask the students what they want to find out about the rain forest. You can whet
   their imaginations with questions such as "Are *all* rain forests hot?" or "What's the
   biggest bug in the rain forest?" Ask them to write their questions on their blue parrot
   shapes and again collect, sort out the duplicates, and attach in the **W**ant to find out
   section.

5. As your class ventures through its rain forest unit, **W**ant to find out questions will be
   answered. Set aside some time every so often to invite students to answer as many of
   the these questions they can. The newly learned facts are then written on green parrot shapes, sorted for duplicates, and attached to the **L**earned section of the KWL
   chart. At the close of your unit, revisit the KWL chart by asking students to help you
   read and celebrate each rain forest fact. Students will be amazed at all they've
   learned.

Canopy Corner
(SCIENCE, ART)

Turn a corner of your classroom into a rain forest. Set up a discovery table decorated to look like a jungle. It's a great place to display rain forest books as well as show off student artwork and reports. Here are some ideas for making your own corner of the jungle.

🍃 **GROW SOME PAPER BAG TREES.** Cut long, wide strips out of brown paper grocery bags. Then staple two or three of these strips together along both long sides and stuff this paper bag "tube" with crumpled newspaper. The tree trunks can be attached to the floor and stacked up and taped all the way to the ceiling. Make thinner ones for branches.

🍃 **HANG AND WRAP VINES.** Heavy twine and twisted strips of green and brown paper make great vines for wrapping around tree trunks. Lichen and moss can be made from lengths of fuzzy yarn strewn over leaves and glued onto trunks.

🍃 **LEAF IT UP.** Cut lots of leaves from green craft paper. Check books for some ideas on different shapes and sizes to make them. The leaves can be attached to vines and branches, hung from the ceiling, and littered around the base of tree trunks.

Let the Canopy Corner grow and change with students' knowledge by adding things used, or made, as you proceed through your rain forest unit, such as rain forest products like tea, coffee beans, cocoa, and rubber; tank bromeliads (page 15) and toucan puppets (page 34). Students can also draw and cut out their favorite rain forest animals from the Jungle Animals ID Cards (page 32) and Forest Dominoes (page 36).

Finding Tropical Rain Forests (GEOGRAPHY)

MATERIALS   globe or world map ♦ reproducible pages 19–20

The world's tropical rain forests lie along the equator mostly within the tropics of Cancer and Capricorn. This activity allows students to explore this for themselves. Start by reviewing the names of the continents, the compass rose, the equator, and the tropics of Cancer and Capricorn on a large map or globe. Point out that although there are cool rain forests, as in the northwestern U.S., the hot tropical ones are located close to the equator. Distribute a copy of page 19 and 20 to students and ask them to answer the questions using their map of rain forests.

EXTENSION ACTIVITY With the help of a globe or map, ask students to fill in the names of the countries where the rain forests are.

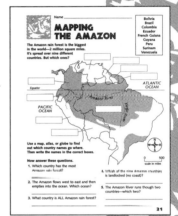

Mapping the Amazon (GEOGRAPHY)

MATERIALS reproducible page 21 ♦ scissors ♦ glue or paste ♦ atlas, globe, or map that shows South American countries clearly ♦ colored pencils

The Amazon rain forest is the world's largest. This activity gives students a closer look at it and helps develop their map skills. Hand out copies of page 21 and help students follow the instructions to complete the page. Invite them to color the map, making the forest green, the rivers blue, and so on. They may add the Andes as well.

EXTENSION ACTIVITY The nine Amazonian countries are all very different. Challenge student groups to choose one of the countries and find out more about it and how its people benefit from—and manage—the resources of the rain forest.

TEACHER TIP
Some students take the lines on maps literally. Explain that we use them to help define particular areas, but that the equator and other lines are only on maps and globes, not on Earth's surface!

AMAZON RIVER FACTS

🍃 The Amazon River is 3,900 miles long. It's the world's second largest river. (The Nile is 4,145 miles long.)

🍃 The Amazon River follows the line of the equator from west to east.

🍃 Because the Amazon is deeper it holds more water than any other river in the world.

🍃 More than 200 smaller rivers flow into the Amazon.

🍃 During the rainy season the Amazon river can rise as much as 45 feet.

🍃 Fish actually swim among the trees when the Amazon floods areas of the rain forest during the rainy season.

🍃 The Amazon is home to the piranha, meat-eating fish.

Green Scene (SCIENCE, MATH)

MATERIALS philodendron plants ◆ notebooks ◆ rulers ◆ watering can

Philodendron is a popular houseplant that grows quickly, and the trailers can easily be coaxed along door frames and walls. Many students are familiar with it, but they may not know that it's a tropical rain forest plant. This activity lets students explore how light affects growth in plants.

1. Divide students into gardening teams. (Each team will need a plant, so vary the team sizes accordingly.) Each team will be responsible for keeping its plant watered and recording the growth in its notebook.

2. Label an equal number of plants: *Shade, Full Sun,* or *Some Sun.* Then give one to each team. Help students to find an appropriate place for their plant's light conditions and ask them to add a team name to the plant's label.

3. Have students set up a chart in their notebooks for recording information about the plant. Have each team record the following starting information:

   🌿 How many shoots are there from the base?

   🌿 How many leaves?

   🌿 How long are the leaves?

   🌿 How long are the trailers?

After students record this information and sketch the plant, ask them to predict in their notebooks how much their plant will have grown in a month (or at the end of your unit). Teams should record their plant's growth every week in the chart. At the end of the unit, the teams can make a simple line graph showing how much or how little their plant grew over time. Were their predictions right? Then have students make a bar graph to compare the different light conditions.

EXTENSION ACTIVITY Challenge teams with the same light conditions to average their data.

Build a Bromeliad (ART)

MATERIALS reproducible page 22 ◆ scissors ◆ green, red, and orange construction paper (or colored-in white paper) ◆ toilet tissue cardboard rolls ◆ tape ◆ glue ◆ crayons or markers

Bromeliads are a kind of epiphyte that have overlapping thick vertical leaves that form a "tank" for holding water. Some can hold as much as ten gallons! The plants not only store water for their own use, but often become a mini-habitat for tadpoles and insects, and a "drinking fountain" for birds, lizards, and even monkeys. In this activity, students create their own tropical bromeliad water tank. The finished bromeliads look great attached to tree trunks of the Canopy Corner!

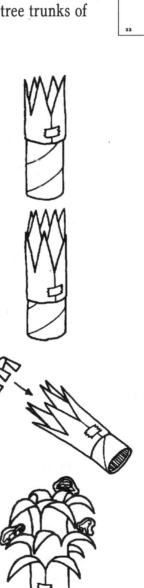

1. Hand out copies of page 22 and ask students to cut out all the patterns.

2. Students take the leaf pattern and trace it onto construction paper. Each student will need one orange, one red, and two green leaf patterns.

3. Pass out the cardboard toilet tissue rolls. Help students wrap and tape the orange leaf pattern around the roll so that it extends beyond the top of the roll.

4. Students wrap and tape the red leaf pattern a little lower down on the roll. They tape it a little more to the right or left of the orange one so that the red leaf tips fall between the orange ones. They do the same with one of the green leaf patterns, taping the pattern a little lower on the roll. The last green leaf pattern should be flush with the bottom of the cardboard roll.

5. Students can curl the leaf points back by carefully wrapping them around a crayon or their fingers. Curl the bottom layer first and work up.

6. Students color the water circle blue and gently push it into the top of the cardboard roll, then glue or tape down the tabs.

7. After coloring the animal visitors, students can cut them out and glue them to the leaves.

How Big Is BIG? (MATH)

MATERIALS butcher paper or oak tag ♦ scissors ♦ masking tape ♦ ruler or tape measure ♦ large paper clips or pennies

FOREST FACT

Rafflesia blossoms can be 3 feet across and weigh 20 pounds!

How many kids can stand on a single flower? A lot if it's a giant rafflesia blossom! Explain that this flower is a yard wide—the largest on earth. Ask the class to predict how many students can fit on it. Note the predictions on the chalkboard, then help students find out how many. Cut a circle of paper three feet wide (you might want to scallop the edges to look more like a flower) and place it on the classroom floor. Have students count aloud as each one joins the crowd on the rafflesia circle until it's full. Were students' predictions close?

FOREST FACT

A python in Malaysia was 32 feet long!

Plants aren't the only giants in the rain forest. Some snakes, such as the anaconda, grow up to 30 feet long and weigh 300 pounds. Ask student groups to mark off on the floor with masking tape how long they think a 30-foot snake would be. Then let them measure their "snakes" and see which group's estimate was the closest.

EXTENSION ACTIVITY Another giant is the 16-inch goliath frog! Cut a 16-inch frog shape from oak tag. The frog pattern to the right will help. Then ask students to predict how many paper clips or pennies they'd need to cover the frog shape. Challenge them to try it and see how close their predictions were.

Rain Forest Layers
(LANGUAGE ARTS)

MATERIALS reproducible pages 23-24 ♦ crayons or markers ♦ scissors

This flap-book will help students visually grasp the differences among the four forest layers—and find out what lives there. Make double-sided copies of pages 23 and 24 and hand one out to each student. Ask students to fold the page in half lengthwise with the pictures on the cover. After coloring the animals and plants, they may cut along the three dotted lines. Then invite them to turn back the flaps to find out more about the layers of the rain forest.

EXTENSION ACTIVITY Divide the class into rain forest research teams and assign each team one of the four rain forest layers. The team's mission is to come up with ways to study the plants and animals of its layer—would explorers need to build skywalks, or use ropes, or could they simply hike to their layer?

Rain Forests, Layers of Life (POSTER)

Invite students to explore the four distinct layers of the rain forest and "meet" some of the creatures that call each home with the Layers of Life poster (bound in this book). To extend learning, have students choose an animal from the poster to research, then report on it. Or place the poster on a table and challenge students to sort their Jungle Animals ID Cards (page 32) and place them on the appropriate layer. Which layer has the most kinds of animals? The least? Why do students think so?

Leafy Critters (ART)

MATERIALS lots of different kinds of leaves ◆ reproducible page 25 ◆ large, heavy paper or cardboard ◆ scissors ◆ glue ◆ google eyes (optional)

Tropical rain forests have an awesome array of plants. But students will be surprised at how many different sizes and shapes of leaves they can find locally. This activity sends students leaf collecting to find leaves to use as art materials.

1. Either ask students to bring in a variety of leaves, or supervise leaf collection as an outdoor activity where students can learn about different plants and trees from the leaves they collect. Remind them that they'll need plenty of small leaves for eyes, ears, and other details.

2. After students have collected the leaves, challenge them to come up with criteria for sorting them, such as size, color, or shape. Then have the class sort all the leaves into the groups.

3. Pass out copies of page 25 and invite students to decide on an animal they want to make as a leafy critter. They may look at the animals on the poster, the Jungle Animals ID Cards, and the Forest Dominoes for ideas.

4. When students know what they want to make, have them arrange different leaves on the page to represent the heads, legs, paws, tails, and other parts of their critters.

5. When they're satisfied with their arrangement, students glue the leaves in place on the paper. (Use large, heavy paper or cardboard for bigger critters.) Students can draw or add google eyes. Ask them to label their critters.

> **TEACHER TIP**
> Before students collect leaves, review some plants they *shouldn't* pick, like poison ivy and poison oak. Show students how to carefully pinch a leaf off of a plant without tearing or damaging the stem.

EXTENSION ACTIVITY Challenge students to look up interesting facts about their critters and write the facts on their papers.

PARROT PATTERN

TROPICAL RAIN FORESTS OF THE WORLD

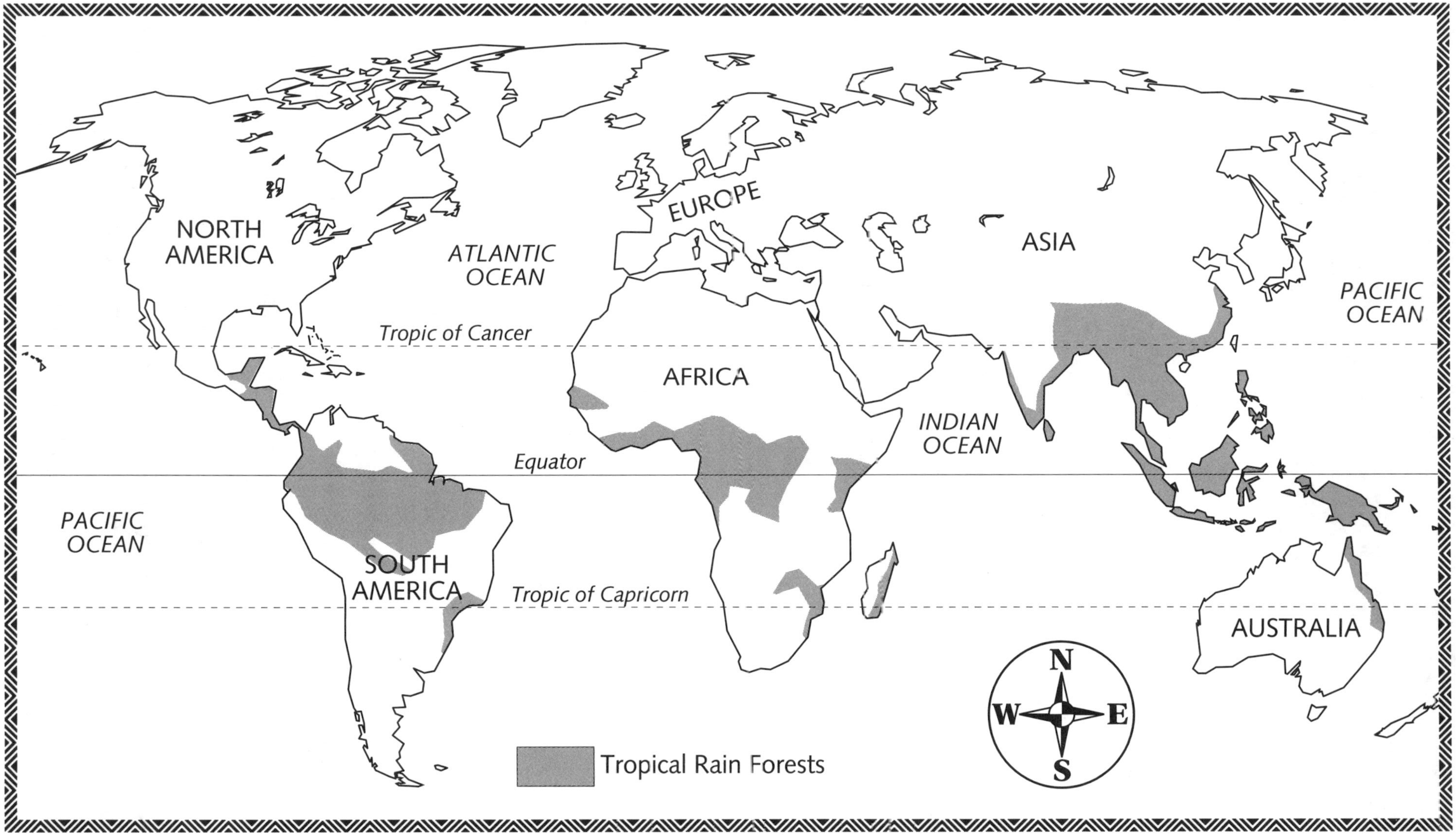

PACIFIC OCEAN

ASIA

INDIAN OCEAN

N E S W

EUROPE

AFRICA

ATLANTIC OCEAN

Tropic of Cancer

Equator

Tropic of Capricorn

AUSTRALIA

SOUTH AMERICA

NORTH AMERICA

PACIFIC OCEAN

Tropical Rain Forests

Name _____

FINDING TROPICAL RAIN FORESTS

**Run your finger along your map's equator.
You just touched most of the world's rain forests!**

**Now answer some questions about these rain forests.
Use your map to find the answers.**

1. Is there a tropical rain forest in Europe? _____

2. Is there a tropical rain forest in the United States?_____

3. Which continent has the biggest rain forest? _____

4. If you wanted to visit every tropical rain forest, how many continents would you

have to go to? _____

5. Where's the rain forest in Asia? In the northern or southern part of the continent?

_____

6. Is Africa's big rain forest on its east or west coast? _____

7. Which two oceans border the rain forests of Asia? _____

_____

8. If a parrot living in California wants to fly to a rain forest, where is the closest one?

_____

9. Which continent has a rain forest the farthest north? _____

10. Which continent has lots of rain forest islands? _____

EXTRA

How much of the whole world—not just the land—is covered in rain forest?
Take a long look at the map and circle your best guess.

(a) 6%   (b) 25%   (c) 60%

Name _____

MAPPING THE AMAZON

Bolivia
Brazil
Colombia
Ecuador
French Guiana
Guyana
Peru
Surinam
Venezuela

The Amazon rain forest is the biggest in the world—2 million square miles. It's spread over nine different countries. But which ones?

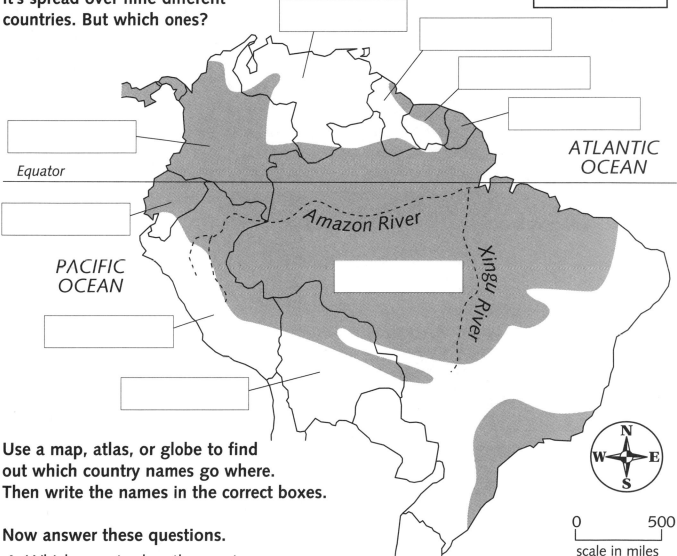

Equator

ATLANTIC OCEAN

Amazon River

Xingu River

PACIFIC OCEAN

N W E S

0   500
scale in miles

Use a map, atlas, or globe to find out which country names go where. Then write the names in the correct boxes.

Now answer these questions.

1. Which country has the most Amazon rain forest?

_____

2. The Amazon flows west to east and then empties into the ocean. Which ocean?

_____

3. What country is ALL Amazon rain forest?

_____

4. Which of the nine Amazon countries is landlocked (no coast)?

_____

5. The Amazon River runs though two countries—which two?

_____

BUILD A BROMELIAD

Cut out all the patterns on this page. Then follow along as your teacher tells you how to put everything together.

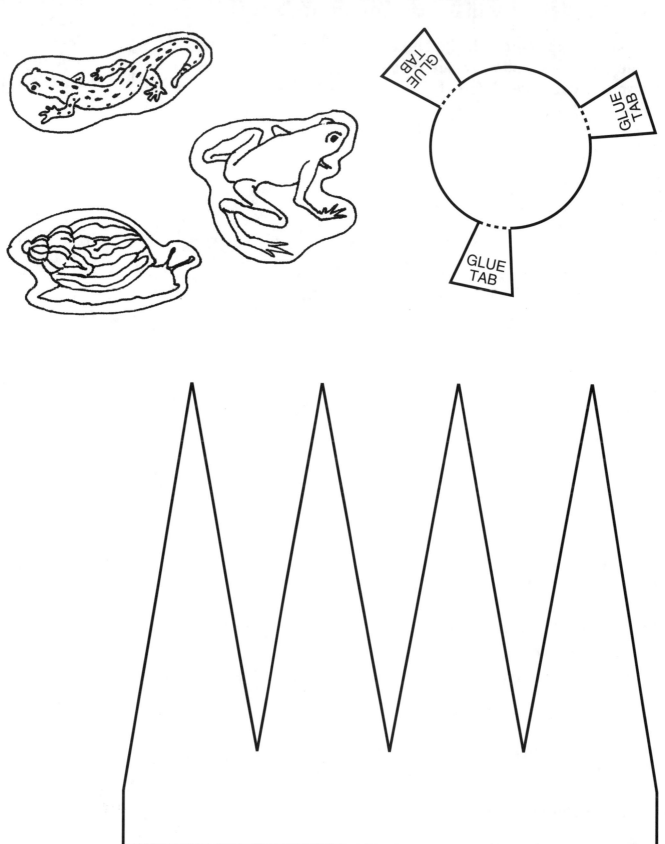

Rain Forest Layers

quetzal

morpho butterfly   squirrel monkey

toucan

bat

sloth

tree boa

jaguar

red-eyed
tree frog

agouti

giant anteater

EMERGENT LAYER

It's the top of the world up here. A few giant trees—some as high as a 15-story building—soak up the most sun. Squirrel monkeys, quetzals, and morpho butterflies live on this layer.

CANOPY

Leafy treetops form a roof over the layers below here. It's a maze of leaves and branches. Sloths, toucans, and bats live here. Why? There are lots of good things to eat!

UNDERSTORY

Less sunshine reaches this far down. So plants grow extra large leaves to catch more light. Snakes, jaguars, and red-eyed tree frogs live here.

FOREST FLOOR

It's dark down here because of all the shade! But giant anteaters and agoutis don't mind. They scramble among ferns, moss, and fallen leaves looking for things to eat on the ground.

Name _____

LEAFY CRITTERS

Did you know that leaves came in so many shapes and sizes? Look what you can make with them! Use this sheet to invent your own leafy critter. When you're done, paste it in place.

ANIMALS, ANIMALS, ANIMALS!

Macaw

Anybody Home?

If you hiked four miles through the dark rain forest floor, you'd probably get a glimpse of only a macaw, maybe a tapir, perhaps some small reptiles, and a few insects like termites and leaf-cutting ants. Since the forest has a wealth of niches, competition for them has resulted in a modest number of individual animals but an enormous number of different species.

The majority of creatures live hidden in the canopy, so on your walk you may hear squawks, howls, and chirps without being able to see the noise-makers, even the ones at ground level. What might you pass in your walk? About 125 mammal species, 400 kinds of birds, 100 species of reptiles, and insects by the thousands.

FOREST FACT
South American macaws are the world's largest parrots.

Profusion in Paradise

Insects, by their sheer numbers, have a greater impact on the forest than any other kind of animal. Billions of them distribute pollen and are an ongoing food source for birds, reptiles, and mammals, as well

FOREST FACT
The Hercules beetle is six inches long!

as one another. Although most invertebrates are small, the warm, stable conditions of the forests have also produced giants: the bird-eating spider is 3 inches across with an 11-inch leg span; the African swallowtail butterfly has a wingspan of 10 inches; the poisonous tiger centipede is more than 10 inches long; and there's a Costa Rican cockroach that would cover an adult's palm!

FOREST FACT
The bird-eating spider is the largest spider in the world.

Amazing Animal Adaptations

While many insects advertise their toxicity with bright colors, others protect themselves by looking like thorns, twigs, or leaves. Some predatory insects use camouflage to ambush prey. One of the most striking is the orchid mantis whose pastel coloring and leg flaps make it look just like its namesake. As insects approach the "flower" for a meal, they often become the meal.

Ants outnumber all other insects in the rain forest. Leaf-cutters are among the most industrious. They snip pieces of leaves and carry them parasol fashion back to nests where they are cleaned, chewed, spit out, and used to cultivate fungus gardens. A single colony of these ants can cut thousands of pounds of leaves in a year.

Some ants actually defend specific plants. For instance, Azteca ants live in crevices of cecropia trees and emerge and sting any animal (including a human) that disturbs the tree. Reciprocating, the tree grows "nectaries" near its leaves, providing food for the ants. Army ants are probably the most fearsome, marching in broad unstoppable columns. The swarm moves at about 70 feet an hour and usually devours anything in its path that isn't quick enough to get away.

Feathers of the Rainbow

Because the canopy is the leafiest layer, it attracts the most insects; therefore, most of the canopy birds are insect eaters. But there are also hundreds of bird species that dine upon the plentiful nectar and fruit.

Toucans with huge multicolored bills and macaws in shocking Day-Glo colors have become symbols of jungles, but they're only the tip of the avian iceberg. There are antbirds that station themselves in front of advancing army ants, not to eat them but to pick off other insects fleeing from the voracious column. There are male bowerbirds who build "bowers" or tunnels of grass in which to court their mates,

Flycatcher

and decorate them with any blue object they can find: bits of glass, flowers, berries, and feathers. The world's largest eagle, the harpy, swoops from the emergent layer and snatches up monkeys and even small antelopes. Another resident is the tiny tailorbird that creates a support for its nest by sewing two sides of a leaf together with "thread" of plant down and spiderweb silk. The sacred bird of the Mayas is the avocado-eating quetzal adorned with emerald green and scarlet feathers and a yard-long tail.

The pitohui of New Guinea is a common jay-size bird known to scientists for more than a hundred years. But just recently they discovered it has a secret weapon—the pitohui's flesh and feathers have a deadly toxin! This protective mechanism is also found half way around the world in the poison arrow frogs of South America.

Flying Snakes and Leaping Lizards

Flying frog

Bats and birds use well-traveled pathways, called flight tunnels, as they fly from tree to tree, and lemurs can leap 300 feet with joyful ease. But there are reptiles and amphibians that do some "flying" of their own. The flying gecko turns into a small glider by spreading flaps of leathery skin along the sides of its body and its webbed feet. If threatened, it parachutes from one tree to the next. Asian flying frogs also glide on four parachutes of skin stretched between the toes of each foot. The paradise flying snake flattens its body by pushing out its ribs and makes its escape by plummeting away from danger. But the ace of reptilian aviators is the small flying dragon, which sails from high branches on winglike flaps of skin stiffened by its ribs. In a clearing, this 8-inch lizard can "fly" nearly 200 feet.

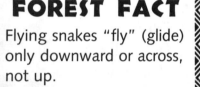

FOREST FACT

Flying snakes "fly" (glide) only downward or across, not up.

The diversity of tropical frogs and toads is amazing! Nowhere else is there such a wide range of size, color, and survival strategies. Horned toads look like dead leaves, while the brilliant colors of tiny poison arrow frogs advertise that they're toxic. Glass frogs are so transparent that their bones, muscles, and internal organs show right through their skin!

Rain forests have more dangerous snakes than other ecosystems but getting a glimpse of them is rare. The dreaded fer-de-lance finds its victims with "pits" (small depressions between eyes and nostrils) that sense the heat generated by warm-blooded prey. Anacondas and pythons are among the largest snakes in the world. Both eat whatever they can coil around and crush—including tapirs, capybaras, and even crocodiles.

Chameleon

Anaconda

Slow loris

Of Aye-Ayes and Marmosets

If asked to name a jungle primate, we may be quick to respond with chimpanzee or spider monkey—but what else? How many of us have ever seen a slow loris, tarsier, ouakari, or macaque? Hundreds of primate species make their home in rain forests. Most have long, strong tails, but the great apes have no tails at all; there are 2-ounce marmosets and 500-pound gorillas, mandrills with bright blue and red facial markings, black and white colobus monkeys, rusty red howlers and orangutans, and golden tamarins. Lemurs, found only in the rain forests of Madagascar, include the rare nocturnal aye-aye and the indri, which makes spectacular leaps through the branches but on the ground hops like a kangaroo.

Tarsier

FOREST FACT

The lemurs are found only in Madagascar.

Ring-tailed lemurs

Rats, Bats, and Cats

Jungle rodents include aquatic rats who feed exclusively on fish, gentle porcupines with prehensile tails, and agoutis that play a significant role in the propagation of certain plants. (They collect and hide many hard-shelled fruits, and the ones they forget to dig up sprout into new plants.) The South American rain forest is also home to the largest rodent in the world—the capybara, which can weigh as much as 100 pounds. Although these plant-eating giants can run like a horse, if pursued, they head for water where their remarkable swimming and diving abilities help them escape.

Capybara

Flying fox

Playing an important role as flower pollinators, nectar-sipping bats thrive in the rain forest, as do the many insect-eating species. There are other bats that only eat frogs, and some that only eat fish. Many bats are fruit eaters, including the large flying fox of Africa, Asia, and Australia. Some of these are the size of small dogs and have five-foot wingspans.

If a design works, why change it? Cats haven't changed much in 40 million years. The number of these stealthy, speedy predators is small, but the diversity of the species is larger here than anywhere else. The biggest wild felines are tigers, jaguars, and leopards. The smaller ones include golden, marbled, and fishing cats, ocelots, and margays. Called the "ghost of Madagascar," the fossa, which looks and behaves like a cat— and was once classified as one—has been moved to the group of animals that includes mongooses and hyenas. Local lore claims that the fossa can make its pupils vanish and that its awful smell is powerful enough to kill a chicken!

Jaguar

Upside-down Slowpoke

There are green insects, birds, and reptiles but no green mammals—with the exception of the greenish looking sloth. The sloth's unusual color comes from algae that grow on its long outer bristlelike fur. Actually, all sorts of tiny creatures live in the sloth's fur. One sloth was found to have three kinds of beetles, six species of mites, and three kinds of moths living in its fur! One of the slowest mammals, it spends most of its life hanging upside down from tree limbs by its hooklike claws. When it comes down to the ground (about once every 10 days), because it can't walk, it drags itself along with its huge claws.

FOREST FACT

It takes a sloth about half an hour to eat one leaf!

ACTIVITIES

Rain Forest Riddles (LANGUAGE ARTS)

MATERIALS reproducible page 39 ◆ scissors ◆ glue ◆ crayons or markers

These riddles make learning about residents of the rain forest fun. Copy and hand out page 39 to students. Read the rhyming riddles aloud with them and then ask students to cut out and color the four animal stamps. Next, students should paste each stamp alongside the riddle that best describes it.

EXTENSION ACTIVITY As children become more familiar with jungle animals, challenge them to invent short riddles of their own.

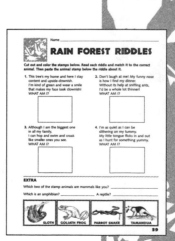

Jungle Animals ID Cards (SCIENCE, ART)

MATERIALS reproducible pages 40–47 ♦ glue or paste ♦ scissors

The cards on pages 40–47 will introduce students to 16 fascinating rain forest creatures. Copy and distribute the sheets to each student. Have them cut out the cards and fold each in half, gluing the two sides together. (Paste the page to heavy paper before cutting and folding to make the cards more durable.) The cards will be used in activities such as Where in the World? and Sorting Out Rain Forest Animals, but you can use the cards in anyother ways you feel are appropriate.

EXTENSION ACTIVITY Many of these rain forest creatures are marvelously colored. Challenge students to find color pictures or photographs of the animals in books and color their cards accordingly.

Where in the World? (GEOGRAPHY)

MATERIALS Jungle Animals ID Cards ♦ globe or map

After students have had some time to look at the Jungle Animals ID Card and read the information, have them try to find each animal's "home" on a globe or map. Ask: *Which animals live the farthest from you? The closest? Which animals could you see if you visited Africa? South America? Asia? Australia?*

Sorting Out Rain Forest Animals

(SCIENCE, MATH)

MATERIALS Jungle Animals ID Cards

The Jungle Animals ID Cards contain a lot of information for students to process. Having student groups sort them in several different ways based on varying criteria is a great way for them to compare and contrast the critters. Challenge your class to come up with some criteria for sorting the animals on there cards. Here are some ideas.

🍂 Ask students to separate the animals on the ID cards according to rain forest layer.

🍂 The animals can also be sorted according to type or *class* of animal, such as mammal, bird, reptile, etc. Ask: *What do all the mammals have in common? The birds? The reptiles? The amphibians?* The What's What sidebar on this page will help.

🍂 Diet is another sorting criterion. Ask students to divide the animals on the cards into: *Herbivores* (fruit and vegetable eaters), *carnivores* (meat eaters) and *omnivores* (everything eaters). Ask: *How many of each eater type are there?*

🍂 Ask students to divide their ID cards by continents. Students may need some help with Madagascar (Africa) and Pacific Islands (Asia).

🍂 Defense strategies of the animals can also be categorized. Which use camouflage? Which have protective scales? Which have "poison" coloring?

EXTENSION ACTIVITY Have students add their own Jungle Animals ID Cards to their collections. You can "white-out" one of the ID cards and then photocopy it for them to use as a template.

WHAT'S WHAT

Mammals are *vertebrates* (having a spinal column). They all feed milk to their young and produce their own body heat (warm-blooded or *endothermic*). Most have fur or hair.

Birds are also warm-blooded vertebrates. They all lay eggs and have feathers, but not all can fly.

Amphibians are vertebrates whose temperature depends on their surroundings (cold-blooded or *ectothermic*). Even the land-dwellers usually return to the water to breed, and their eggs hatch as larvae.

Reptiles are ectothermic vertebrates, most of which lay eggs. Their scaly skin keeps them from drying out, so they spend more time on land than amphibians do.

Arthropods are egg-laying *invertebrates* (without backbones). Insects, spiders, and scorpions are all arthropods.

Treetop Toucan (ART)

MATERIALS reproducible page 48 ◆ construction paper ◆ glue or paste ◆ markers ◆ scissors ◆ brass paper fasteners ◆ tape ◆ craft stick

On page 48 you'll find an easy pattern as well as diagrams for making a toucan puppet that can open its huge bill. Students can use their puppets as cast members in the play *Too Many Toucans!* (page 50) or in story plays of their own. Photocopy and distribute page 48 to students and help them follow these assembly directions.

DIRECTIONS

1. Glue page 48 to construction paper.

2. Color the toucan and the bill section of the other piece. Students can use the poster or pictures in books as a coloring guide. Remind them that the color pattern of each toucan's bill is different, which helps them recognize one another. Encourage them to draw unique bills.

3. Cut out both parts along the dark solid lines.

4. Push a brass fastener through the star on the toucan and then through the star on the other piece as shown. Fold back the fastener tabs.

5. Tape a craft stick to the back of the branch, overlapping the tail as shown. Be sure the tail can still slide back and forth.

8. Hold the craft stick in one hand. Move the tail back and forth with the other to make the toucan open and close its beak.

EXTENSION ACTIVITY Explain that toucans are very playful birds that often play "catch" with pieces of fruit. Divide the class into three teams. Give each team a single link of paper chain to be placed on the bottom half of the first toucan puppet's bill. The teams can have a relay race in which they pass the link from toucan to toucan without dropping it.

Henry the Boa (ART)

MATERIALS reproducible page 49 ◆ heavy paper ◆ scissors ◆ glue ◆ tape ◆ markers ◆ craft sticks ◆ google eyes

Page 49 includes the pattern for making a boa puppet—and fun facts about boa constrictors. The snake may be used as a puppet in the play *Too Many Toucans!* on page 50, as well as a slinky resident of your Canopy Corner. Copy and hand out the page to all students and help them assemble their puppets following the directions below.

DIRECTIONS

1. Paste the pattern to heavy paper.

2. Color the boa constrictor. Refer to pictures in books as a coloring guide.

3. Cut out the snake along the solid line.

4. Paste a google eye in place on the snake's head.

5. Tape a craft stick handle to the snake's back.

Too Many Toucans! (LANGUAGE ARTS, DRAMA)

MATERIALS reproducible page 50 ◆ toucan and boa puppets (optional)

In this short play, five toucans whine about being crowded. They all complain that there are too many of them in the tree—until a boa makes a threatening appearance, and the birds discover that there are times when "too many" can be just the right amount. Give students the play on page 50. They can read it aloud or enact the roles using their toucan and boa puppets (pages 48 and 49). After they've read the play, invite students to draw a picture about the story.

EXTENSION ACTIVITY

Divide students into groups and challenge them to come up with new adventures for the toucans and boas. They may perform their short skits for the rest of the class.

Finding Frogs (PUZZLE)

MATERIALS reproducible page 51

There are more kinds of frogs in rain forests than any other place in the world. Scientists that study frogs and other kinds of amphibians and reptiles are still discovering new kinds of frogs in the rain forest. The reproducible on page 51 gives students the opportunity to discover some frogs too. They'll really have to look hard to find the 20 frogs hiding in the rain forest!

EXTENSION ACTIVITY When students have found all 20 frogs, challenge them to color the frogs based on pictures of real rain forest frogs and then label them.

Forest Dominoes (SCIENCE)

MATERIALS reproducible pages 52-53 ◆ glue ◆ scissors ◆ markers ◆ heavy paper or poster board ◆ penny

Pages 52-53 assemble into domino playing pieces that will introduce students to the main animal groups. Copy and distribute the sheets and ask students to paste them onto heavy paper or poster board. Invite students to color the pictures and then cut out each domino piece. Ask: *Which of the Forest Domino animals are mammals? What is a mammal? Which are reptiles? What is a reptile?* and so on. The What's What sidebar on page 33 will help. Next, divide students into pairs to play Forest Dominoes! (One pair needs a single set of Forest Dominoes.)

HOW TO PLAY

1. Turn all the dominoes picture side down. Each player picks and keeps four dominoes but doesn't show them to his or her opponent.

2. Flip a penny to see who will go first—heads wins. The first player (player A) places a domino on the table, picture side up.

3. In order to lay down a domino, player B must be able to match mammal to mammal, bird to bird, etc. If player B can't do that, he or she must choose a remaining domino until a domino is drawn that can be played.

4. Players take turns laying down dominoes and or drawing from the pile until someone gets rid of all of his or her dominoes—the winner! If, at the end, neither player can play his or her remaining dominoes, the one with the fewest dominoes left is the winner.

Rain Forest Resident Research Report
(SCIENCE, WRITING)

MATERIALS reproducible page 54 ◆ encyclopedias, rain forest reference books

The Forest Dominoes feature 36 rain forest residents that students can learn more about. Either assign or allow students to select one of the Forest Domino animals, making sure there's no duplication. Then, distribute page 54 to students. Challenge them to find the needed information to complete the page in classroom reference books and/or the library. When they've finished their investigation and answered the questions, invite them to read their reports to their classmates, who can follow along with their sets of dominoes.

Rain Forest Rainbow Book
(ART, SCIENCE)

MATERIALS drawing paper ◆ markers ◆ hole punch ◆ yarn or string

To create a class book of rain forest animals, ask each student to contribute one or two drawings of brightly colored creatures, such as Madagascar day gecko, macaw, or golden lion marmoset. Explain that they can find pictures and diagrams of the animals they want to draw in reference books and nature magazines. Suggest that they use markers and that they label the picture with the animal's name and where it lives. Bind the collection and title it "Rain Forest Rainbow." Display this book when the class holds a rain forest *moka* (celebration) and "open house" for other classes.

EXTENSION ACTIVITIES Several of the class projects, such as the research reports and collections of rain forest riddles, can be bound with title pages and displayed on the Discovery Table under the Canopy. Other class publications can include students' poems, plays, and stories.

What's for Lunch? (SCIENCE)

MATERIALS reproducible page 55 and 56 ◆ heavy paper or poster board ◆ paste or glue ◆ scissors

There are ten hungry animals. But which will eat and which will be eaten? Students find out in this game that teaches the basic food chain concept. The animal squares are numbered 1 to 10, with number 10 (jaguar) at the top of the food chain, and number 1 (fly) at the bottom. The higher an animal is on the food chain, the more animals it gets to eat for lunch. For instance, if one player turns over a coatimundi (8) and one a toad (3) card, the toad is lunch and the player is out of the game.

1. Photocopy and distribute pages 55 and 56. Have students paste the pages to heavy paper and then cut out the animal cards.

2. Have students to choose a partner. The players place their cards face down between them.

3. Each player turns over a card. The animal with the higher number eats the lower-numbered animal. The player with the higher number wins the round and keeps those two cards.

4. Students continue for five rounds. The player with the most cards wins the game.

EXTENSION ACTIVITY Pairs of students can also play Concentration with two combined sets of cards. One player turns over two cards. If they match, he or she keeps them and goes again. If not, they are turned back over and it's the other player's turn to try. The player with the most cards at the end wins.

Meet the Cloudrunner (CRITICAL THINKING)

MATERIALS reproducible page 57

Who would have imagined that in 1996 scientists would discover a new species of mammal? A squirrel-size mammal was recently discovered in the rain forest tree tops of Panay, a Philippine island. It's been given the name Cloudrunner, weighs about two pounds, has a tail longer than its body, and seldom leaves its den during the day—it's nocturnal. Not much else about it is known. Include students in this amazing scientific finding by inviting them to make guesses about this mysterious new mammal. Copy and hand out page 57. Challenge students to answer as many of the questions as they can.

RAIN FOREST RIDDLES

Cut out and color the stamps below. Read each riddle and match it to the correct animal. Then paste the animal stamp below the riddle about it.

1. This tree's my home and here I stay
content and upside-downish.
I'm kind of green and wear a smile
that makes my face look clownish!
WHAT AM I?

2. Don't laugh at me! My funny nose
is how I find my dinner.
Without its help at sniffing ants,
I'd be a whole lot thinner!
WHAT AM I?

3. Although I am the biggest one
in all my family,
I can hop and swim and croak
like smaller ones you see.
WHAT AM I?

4. I'm as quiet as I can be
slithering on my tummy.
My little tongue flicks in and out
as I hunt for something yummy.
WHAT AM I?

EXTRA

Which two of the stamp animals are mammals like you? _____

Which is an amphibian? _____ A reptile? _____

| SLOTH | GOLIATH FROG | PARROT SNAKE | TAMANDUA |

SLOTH

SLOTH
Class: mammal
Home: Central and South America
Layer: canopy
Food: fruit and leaves

◆ A sloth spends most of its time hanging upside down from branches.

◆ It moves so slowly that it takes a *whole day* to move to another tree.

◆ A sloth can climb and even swim, but it can't walk! On the ground, it drags itself along with its claws.

◆ Insects graze on the green algae growing on the sloth's fur.

◆ One sloth had 170 moths and 978 beetles living in its fur.

POISON ARROW FROG

POISON ARROW FROG
Class: amphibian
Home: South America
Layer: forest floor and understory
Food: insects

◆ Most kinds of poison arrow frogs are small enough to sit on a penny.

◆ Their brilliant colors warn predators, "Don't eat me! I'm poisonous!"

◆ The parents will climb a tree carrying their tadpoles on their backs. When they reach a bromeliad plant, they set the tadpoles free in a pool of water.

◆ Indians of the rain forest use the frogs' poison on the tips of their hunting arrows.

JUNGLE ANIMALS ID CARDS

ANACONDA

Class: reptile
Home: South America
Layer: forest floor
Food: animals

- An anaconda belongs to the boa family. It can grow up to 30 feet long and weigh more than 300 pounds.
- This snake spends a lot of time swimming and floating in slow-moving water.
- It eats whatever it can encircle and squeeze to death—even crocodiles!
- It may take weeks for it to digest a large meal.
- A female gives birth to about 50 live young at a time. Each one is almost 2 feet long!

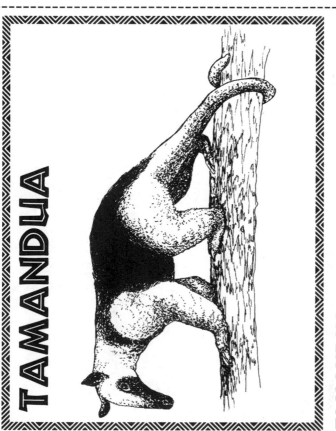

TAMANDUA

Class: mammal
Home: Central and South America
Layer: canopy
Food: ants, termites, bees

- The tamandua's nickname is "stinker of the forest" because it can smell awful.
- A baby is carried piggyback until it's almost as big as its mother.
- A tamandua's mouth is no bigger around than the top of a pencil.
- It catches insects with its long sticky tongue.
- A tamandua stands upright like a bear when it's scared.

JAGUAR

JAGUAR

Class: mammal
Home: Central and South America
Layer: forest floor and understory
Food: animals

- ◆ A jaguar looks like a big leopard. It's the largest American wild cat and weighs about 300 pounds.
- ◆ It isn't a social animal, and it goes out of its way to avoid fights.
- ◆ It's the only big cat that doesn't roar.
- ◆ Jaguars are super swimmers and often hunt in the water. They catch large fish, turtles, and even alligators.
- ◆ A female jaguar has up to four cubs at a time. They stay with her until they're two years old.

FLYING FOX

FLYING FOX

Class: mammal
Home: Africa, Asia, and Australia
Layer: canopy
Food: fruit, nectar, flowers

- ◆ This 2-pound bat has a wingspan of nearly 5 feet!
- ◆ It doesn't use sonar to find its food like nighttime bats do. It's awake during the day to fly around and uses its eyes and nose to find food.
- ◆ This bat sleeps in trees instead of caves.
- ◆ The flying fox's wings have "elbows" that can fold up and wrap around it like a cape.
- ◆ It helps the plants it visits by pollinating their flowers and spreading their seeds.

SHORT-HORNED CHAMELEON

SHORT-HORNED CHAMELEON

Class: reptile
Home: Madagascar
Layer: understory
Food: insects

◆ A chameleon's eyes move separately. It can look in two directions at once.

◆ It can change its color to match its surroundings. That way it's hidden from prey and predators.

◆ Its sticky tongue is often longer than its whole body. It shoots it out to catch bugs with lightning speed.

◆ This lizard can raise up skin flaps on the back of its head like elephant ears.

BABIRUSA

BABIRUSA

Class: mammal
Home: Pacific Islands
Layer: forest floor
Food: berries, roots, bulbs

◆ This strange-looking wild pig is pretty much naked. It has almost no hair or fur.

◆ Babirusas always give birth to twins.

◆ A babirusa's superlong tusks are a mystery. Scientists don't know what the animal uses them for.

◆ An old legend says that babirusas hang from branches by their tusks when they sleep.

◆ This animal easily swims from one island to another.

JUNGLE ANIMALS ID CARDS

GIANT PANGOLIN

Class: mammal
Home: Africa and Asia
Layer: forest floor
Food: termites and ants

- It's also called the "scaly anteater." It uses its huge claws to tear into termite mounds.
- Such big claws get in the way of normal walking. So the pangolin has to walk on its knuckles.
- It has tiny eyes and no teeth but a great sense of smell.
- When a pangolin sees danger it rolls itself into a tight ball and wraps its tail around its body for protection. Predators can be badly cut by the razor-sharp tail scales.
- The pangolin has thick eyelids and can close up its ears and nose. This protects it when the ants start biting.

OKAPI

Class: mammal
Home: Central Africa
Layer: forest floor
Food: leaves and grass

- People used to think an okapi was a kind of wild horse. But it's really related to the giraffe.
- It lives alone or in pairs, but never in big herds.
- Baby okapis have manes that disappear by the time they're grown up.
- An okapi doesn't see very well. But it has a super sense of hearing and smell.
- It pulls leaves from trees with its blue-black tongue, which is so long it can clean any part of its body.

TARSIER

TARSIER

Class: mammal
Home: Asia
Layer: understory
Food: lizards, insects, small fish and crabs

◆ This tiny night animal has the largest eyes in the jungle. But it finds its food by listening with its paper-thin ears.

◆ Its eyes are too big to move. But it can turn its head all the way around like an owl.

◆ The kitten-size tarsier leaps like a kangaroo.

◆ Its fingers and toes have sticky pads at the tips.

◆ It grabs insects with both hands and then *munches.*

HOWLER MONKEY

HOWLER MONKEY

Class: mammal
Home: South America
Layer: emergent and canopy
Food: fruits, nuts, buds, blossoms

◆ The howler is the biggest monkey in South America.

◆ It's also the noisiest animal in the rain forest. Its hoots and howls can be heard for *miles.*

◆ Howlers live in groups of up to 30 animals. Every morning they ROAR! to warn others to keep off their territory.

◆ The howler doesn't jump much. It's slower than most monkeys and uses its tail like an extra arm.

◆ A mom howler has one baby at a time and carries it in her arms or on her back until it's a year old.

JUNGLE ANIMALS ID CARDS

TOUCAN

Class: bird
Home: Central and South America
Layer: emergent and upper canopy
Food: fruit, frogs, insects

◆ A toucan's bill is very light because it's hollow. It's made of the same material as your fingernails, keratin.

◆ There's a different pattern on each bill which helps toucans tell one another apart.

◆ Toucans live in small flocks and are very playful. They like to play "catch" with pieces of fruit.

◆ A toucan's foot is like a woodpecker's. Two toes face front and two face back.

KINKAJOU

Class: mammal
Home: South America
Layer: emergent and canopy
Food: fruit and occasionally insects

◆ The soft, woolly kinkajou looks a lot like a monkey, but it's really a cousin of the raccoon.

◆ It spends all its time in trees. It sleeps in safe tree hollows during the day.

◆ Kinkajous are awake and busy at night. They look for sweet fruit and crunchy bugs.

◆ People in South America often keep the cat-size animal as a pet. It's smart and friendly.

◆ A kinkajou's tail is twice as long as its body. It can grab onto things.

GORILLA

Class: mammal
Home: Africa
Layer: forest floor and understory
Food: leaves and fruit

◆ This is the largest ape in the world. A male can weigh 500 pounds and stand nearly 6 feet tall!

◆ Although it can look and sound scary, the gorilla is a very gentle, shy animal.

◆ Gorillas live in small groups that are led by an old male. He's called a silverback after the gray hair on his back.

◆ A gorilla has a good sense of smell and hearing. But it has *super* eyesight.

◆ Every night gorillas make a new "bed" out of leafy branches.

HARPY EAGLE

Class: bird
Home: South America
Layer: emergent
Food: animals

◆ The harpy stands over three feet tall. It's the largest eagle in the world.

◆ It takes a month for a pair of harpy eagles to make a nest. They build it on top of a very tall tree. They keep adding twigs and leaves to it every year until it's *huge.*

◆ Harpies hatch only a single egg every other year. The chick stays with its parents for a whole year.

◆ Harpies are so strong that they can swoop down into the canopy and carry off monkeys, sloths—and even small antelopes.

TREETOP TOUCAN PUPPET PATTERN

Paste this page onto heavy paper and cut out the pieces. Your teacher will help you put it together.

HENRY THE BOA

Paste this page onto heavy paper and cut it out. Your teacher will help you put it together.

FUN FACTS ABOUT BOAS

- Boa constrictors can grow up to 18 feet in length.
- The boa uses its strong tail to grab on to branches—just like a monkey.
- When a boa rests, its body hangs in loops over a tree branch so that when it sees a meal, it can quickly straighten out and catch its victim.
- Boas have tiny holes in their lips that can sense an animal's body heat. Even in the dark, they can find a warm, furry meal.
- Tree boas hardly ever leave their trees except when they go for a quick swim in a jungle river.
- Dinner for a boa includes rats and bats. And the emerald tree boa can catch birds as they fly by.
- Boas can only make one sound—a hiss.

TOO MANY TOUCANS!

CAST: 5 Toucans: Tilly, Thomas, Tessa, Timothy, and Topper
1 Boa: Henry

SCENE: *All the toucans are crowded next to one another on a branch. They all face the same way and pluck berries from the same nearby branch.*

TILLY: *(Bumping shoulders)* Move over, Timothy! You're crowding me!

TIMOTHY: *(Bumping Thomas, the next in line)* Are you a toucan or a cuckoo, Tilly? Can't you see there's nowhere for me to move? There are too many toucans in this tree!

THOMAS: Watch it, Timothy, there isn't enough room on this branch! *(As he leans over to pluck a berry, he bumps the next bird in line.)* Move over, Tessa, I need a little space! There are too many toucans in this tree!

TESSA: *(bumping Topper)* Bicker, bicker, bicker! Just too many toucans in this tree! Move over, Topper!

TOPPER: I am over, Tessa! One more inch and I'll be in another tree!

TILLY: Good idea, Topper, I'm being squashed! There are just too many toucans in this tree!

All the birds bump and jostle one another, but stubbornly remain on the same branch.

THOMAS: We're so crowded we're like sardines in a can!

TIMOTHY: Like bees in a hive!

TILLY: Like bugs in a rug!

TESSA: Like peas in a pod!

TOPPER: Uh-oh! Does anybody see what I see? Here comes hungry Henry, slithering up the trunk!

All the toucans glare as Henry crawls closer and closer. All at once they squawk loudly and leave the branch to dive at the big boa. Each one takes little pecks at the snake until it gives up in disgust and slithers away.

TIMOTHY: *(to the retreating snake)* Bye-bye, Henry! Don't hurry back!

HENRY: Don't worry. There are TOO MANY TOUCANS in this tree for me!

All the birds return to the branch, squeezing into their original places.

TILLY: *(plucking a berry)* Just what I always said: There can never be too many toucans in a tree!

THOMAS: How true!

TESSA: It's friendly like this!

TIMOTHY: It's cozy like this!

TOPPER: And it's a lot safer like this!

50

Name _____

BE A FROG FINDER!

What place has the most kinds of frogs? The rain forest!
Scientists discover new kinds of frogs there all the time. This
picture has 20 frogs hiding in the rain forest. So start searching!
When you find a frog, outline it with a pencil. Good luck!

FOREST DOMINOES

These two pages have 36 different animals on 18 domino pieces.
Paste each page onto heavy paper and then cut the dominoes out.

CHAMELEON 
reptile

mammal 
ROYAL ANTELOPE

BUSHBABY 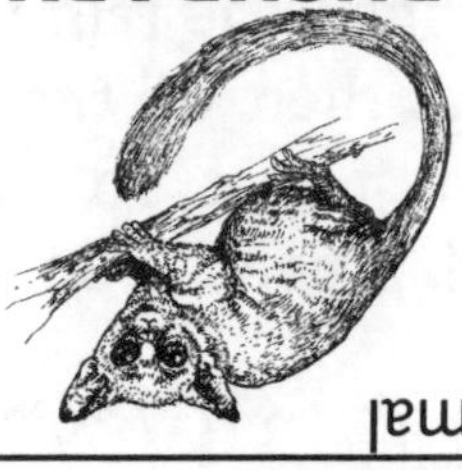
mammal

bird 
ANTBIRD

LEMUR 
mammal

bird 
HARPY EAGLE

FLYING FROG 
amphibian

mammal 
CAPYBARA

PANGOLIN 
mammal

reptile 
PARROT SNAKE

BIRD-EATING SPIDER 
arthropod

mammal 
DIANA MONKEY

TAPIR 
mammal

mammal 
KINKAJOU

ATLAS MOTH 
arthropod

bird 
TROGON

WALKING LEAF 
arthropod

mammal 
PORCUPINE

FOREST DOMINOES

CROCODILE	STICK INSECT	HERCULES BEETLE
reptile	arthropod	arthropod
mammal	bird	mammal
LORIS	MACAW	MONGOOSE

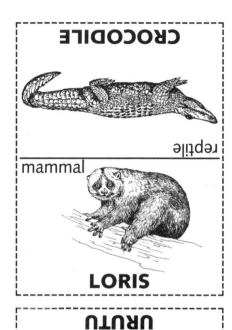
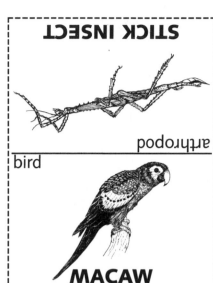
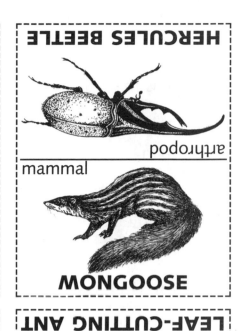

URUTU	AGOUTI	LEAF-CUTTING ANT
reptile	mammal	arthropod
mammal	reptile	mammal
MOONRAT	YELLOW-LEGGED TORTOISE	TAMANDUA

GOLIATH FROG	TREE FROG	POISON ARROW FROG
amphibian	amphibian	amphibian
mammal	bird	mammal
GORILLA	HOATZIN	CUSCUS

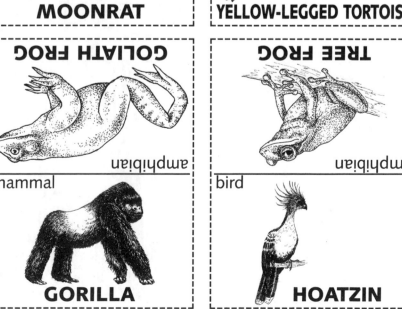
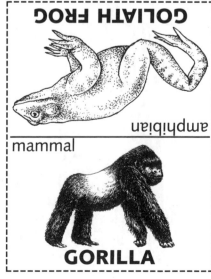

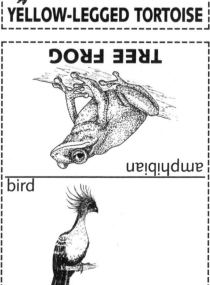

Name _____

RAIN FOREST RESIDENT RESEARCH REPORT

1. What is this animal called? _____

2. What kind of animal is it? (check one)

☐ bird ☐ mammal ☐ reptile

☐ arthropod ☐ amphibian

3. In which rain forest does it live?

_____

4. Which rain forest layer does it like best? (check one)

☐ emergent ☐ canopy

☐ understory ☐ forest floor

5. What does it eat? _____

_____

6. One of its enemies is: _____

7. What neat things can it do? _____

_____

_____

Draw a picture of it.

WHAT'S FOR LUNCH?

What eats what? Find out by playing this game. First paste these pages onto heavy paper. Then cut out the ten cards along the dashed lines.

JAGUAR 10

HARPY EAGLE 9

COATIMUNDI 8

TEGUS 7

VIPER 6

WHAT'S FOR LUNCH?

BIRD-EATING SPIDER 10

FLYCATCHER 4

TOAD 3

MANTIS 2

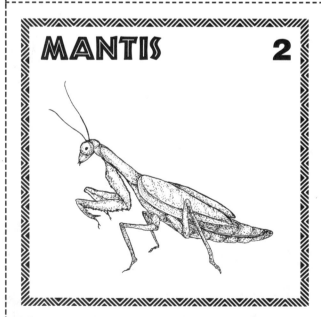

FLY 1

Name _____

MEET THE CLOUDRUNNER

Scientists just discovered this animal in the Philippine rain forest! Because it's new to us, not much is known about it yet.

Take a good look at the cloudrunner and try to answer the questions.

1. What kind of animal do you think it is? (check one)

   ☐ bird   ☐ mammal

   ☐ reptile   ☐ arthropod

   ☐ amphibian

2. What do you think it eats? _____

   _____

3. How do you think it got its name? _____

   _____

4. When do you think it's awake and busy? Day or night? _____

   Why? _____

   _____

5. What other animal does cloudrunner remind you of?_____

   Why? _____

   _____

_____

EXTRA

Why do you think no one knew about it until now? _____

_____

_____

PEOPLE AND PRODUCTS

Rain forest products are part of our daily lives: the *rubber* garden hose we use to water the lawn, the *coffee* and *tea* we drink, the *chocolate* and *cashews* we snack on, the *banana* we slice onto our cereal, and many of the *medicines* that heal us. We tie our old newspapers with *jute*; we set our tables with *rattan* place mats, sprinkle *paprika* on the pot roast, and rub *coconut oil* on our skin. Most of us probably use dozens of rain forest products every day.

Tropical Supermarket

Three very popular beverages in this country—coffee, tea, and cola—all originated in rain forests. Without the forests' flavorful bounty, we never would have enjoyed bananas, pineapples, chocolate, vanilla, avocados, Brazil nuts, black pepper, coconut, or even chewing gum. Although today most of our citrus fruits come from Florida or California, grapefruits, oranges, limes, and lemons originated in the rain forests. Today, many of the popular forest foods are farm grown, but the wild plants still exist—and they're very important. If a particular crop is susceptible to disease, scientists can cross wild strains with the cultivated one to make the domestic crop stronger and more disease resistant.

Brazil nut

Fiber, Sap, and Oil

Tropical plant fibers are used to make cord, soundproofing, and packaging. Palm fibers are used to make chair seats, window blinds, and baskets. The sap of many tropical plants is an essential element in a number of foods. The best known sap is the latex used to produce rubber, but another latex sap from sapodilla trees is used in chewing gum. Various tree resins are used to make varnish and enamels, while oils obtained from forest plants are used in medicines, soaps, cosmetics, candles, and cooking. Certain roots and flowers provide us with natural insecticides, and seeds from urucú trees give us annatto, a food colorant in cheese, baked goods, soups, and sauces.

Medical Secrets

Perhaps the most important benefit we reap from rain forests is medicine. We've used ipecac, quinine, and many others for some time. Recently, the rosy periwinkle of Madagascar's jungle has been found effective in treating Hodgkin's disease and childhood leukemia.

Witch doctors, medicine men, *curanderos,* and shamans of the rain forests never attended medical school. Their knowledge comes from more than 200 generations of experimentation with local plants. These days, scientists from all over the world are enlisting the shamans' help in finding plants with healing properties. The race is on—with the forests disappearing at an alarming rate and old shamans dying off, ethnobotanists (scientists who study the relationship between plants and people) need to understand the ways native people utilize their environment. We have, after all, tested less than 1 percent of the 250,000 rain forest plants for medical applications. From that tiny sampling we've derived 25 percent of all our prescription medicines. What new wonder drugs might still be found?

Living in the Rain Forests

About a thousand indigenous tribes live in the world's remaining rain forests, continuing to survive in much the same way as their ancestors did for thousands of years. They know how to find and hunt game animals; they know which fruits are sweet and juicy and which provide poison for their hunting arrows; they know which plants yield medicines for healing wounds, curing leg cramps, and easing childbirth; they know which materials work best for building shelters and canoes. Most important, these people understand that if they destroy their environment, it will no longer support their needs.

Natives of the rain forest obtain most of their food by hunting and gathering. Farming is on a very small scale, intended to fill only the needs of the farmer's family. Because the number of indigenous people is low, they can use slash-and-burn methods to clear land for their tiny farms. After using an area for a few years, they move on and let the soil "rest" for about 20 years before planting it again. During these "unused" years, the forest replenishes itself. These people may never have heard the phrase "sustainable agriculture," yet that's exactly what they practice.

Rain Forest Peoples

The Mbuti, Baka, and Efe people of central Africa consider the forest their "protector." Although they interact with people in outside villages, bartering meat for tools and other products, they dislike venturing out of the forest. They find the heat oppressive, don't trust the water, and often become listless and sickly. According to anthropologist Colin Turnbull, as soon as they return to the forest, they quickly recover.

The Thai rain forest is home to the Lua people; the Penan populate what little is left of the Borneo forest; and the Yakuno and Kayapo Indians live along the Amazon river. The Maya people, many of whom still live in the forests of Central America, once flourished within a complex and culturally rich society that had a written language, mathematics, and masterful architecture.

ACTIVITIES

Rain Forest Treasure Hunt (SCIENCE, MATH)

MATERIALS reproducible page 63

This activity will let students discover how many rain forest products are right under their noses. Copy and pass out page 63 for students to take home. After they have checked off what they found at home, do a classwide tally of all the products on the chalkboard. When the tallying is finished, ask: *What was the most common product found in your homes? The least common?* Challenge the class to create a bar graph of the top five or ten products.

EXTENSION ACTIVITY Divide students into graphing groups and assign each group one of the categories on the reproducible: Rain Forest Spices, Foods From The Forest, or Useful Things. The student groups then make a bar graph of all the items in their category using the classroom tally numbers. Have the groups present their findings to the class.

Jungle Products Poster (SCIENCE)

MATERIALS magazines ◆ supermarket flyers ◆ scissors ◆ poster board or oak tag ◆ glue ◆ markers ◆ reproducible page 64

Making a poster of rain forest-based products is a great way to demonstrate how rain forests fit into students' daily lives.

DIRECTIONS

1. Divide students into groups and challenge them to find and clip as many pictures of rain forest products from magazines and supermarket flyers as they can. If they can't find a picture of something they're looking for, encourage them to draw it.

2. When groups have collected or drawn enough pictures, invite them to sort the pictures into several categories of their choosing, such as rubber products, medicines, or foods.

3. Each group now puts it all together into an attractive and informative poster. Encourage them to put like items together under that category's label. And don't forget a title.

4. To finish the poster, give students copies of page 64 and have them cut out and color the leaf shapes. These can be glued to the edges of the poster to create a jungle setting or frame.

The Shaman's Advice (LANGUAGE ARTS)

MATERIALS reproducible pages 65–66 ♦ stapler

Many rain forest peoples tell folktales about their animal neighbors that share the forest. One such story is about the ocelot, a cat that lives in the Amazon rain forest of South America. During the day the ocelot stays hidden, but at night it comes out to hunt for food. The beautiful black markings on its golden-yellow coat help it to blend in with the surrounding forest, thus making it easier for it to stalk prey without being seen. How did the ocelot get those handy spots? The folktale in this mini-book offers an explanation. Follow the instructions below to assemble the mini-books.

DIRECTIONS

1. Make double-sided copies of pages 65 and 66 and hand them out to the class.

2. Begin with the side that shows panels D, C, B, and A facing up.

3. Cut the four panels apart along the solid lines.

4. Next, place the panels on top of one another in alphabetical order, with panel A on top.

5. Staple the book along the dashed line and fold.

Invite beginning readers to use picture clues to help them understand the text. Ask fluent readers to stop reading halfway through and to predict: *What will happen when the ocelot follows the shaman's advice?* After they finish the folktale, ask: *Were you right?*

EXTENSION ACTIVITY After students read the folktale, challenge them to stretch their imaginations and invent other stories to explain the ocelot's markings. They can carry this farther by creating stories to explain the lemur's ringed tail or the toucan's rainbow-colored bill.

Papua Painted Mask (ART)

MATERIALS reproducible page 67 ◆ heavy paper or poster board ◆ glue or paste ◆ crayons or markers ◆ scissors ◆ tape ◆ craft stick

The indigenous people of New Guinea paint their faces as part of the celebration of special occasions like weddings or other special family events. Photocopy and distribute page 67. Draw students' attention to the small pictures at the bottom of the page. These are some examples of how they paint their faces. Explain that different events call for faces to be painted in different ways. But all seem to include red as a major color. White, blue, and black are also commonly used. Invite students to make a mask for themselves.

DIRECTIONS

1. Paste page 67 to a piece of heavy paper.

2. Challenge students to decide what occasion their masks will be for. A wedding? A feast? A new baby? Ask them to write this on their paper.

3. Invite students to draw designs on their masks. You can remind them of the New Guineans' color schemes and patterns, but they shouldn't feel limited by them.

4. When the mask is finished, cut it out—don't forget the eyeholes.

5. Tape the craft stick to the back of the mask for a handle.

The masks make great additions to your Canopy Corner and are required attire for the rain forest celebration or *moka* on page 73.

EXTENSION ACTIVITY Help students design ocelot masks—some with spots, and some without. Then, after making and reading *The Shaman's Advice* on pages 65-66, they can use the masks to help act out the story.

Name _____

THERE'S A JUNGLE IN MY HOUSE!

Parts of the rain forest are as close as your home! Want to find them? Look for the rain forest products below at home. Put a check mark next to everything you find.

Rain Forest Spices

- [ ] allspice
- [ ] cayenne
- [ ] chili pepper
- [ ] cinnamon
- [ ] ginger
- [ ] nutmeg
- [ ] black pepper
- [ ] vanilla

Foods from the Forest

- [ ] avocado
- [ ] banana
- [ ] cashew nuts
- [ ] cocoa
- [ ] coconut
- [ ] coffee
- [ ] lemon
- [ ] lime
- [ ] orange
- [ ] pineapple

Useful Things

- [ ] balsa wood
- [ ] balloon
- [ ] bamboo
- [ ] jute (twine)
- [ ] rattan
- [ ] rubber ball
- [ ] rubber band
- [ ] rubber stamp
- [ ] pencil eraser

LEAFY FRAME

These leaf patterns are shaped like rain forest plants. Color and cut them out. Use them to decorate or frame your Jungle Products Poster.

Once there was a yellow cat who could hardly catch enough to eat. It grew weak and skinny. Then it heard of a wise old shaman who lived deep in the forest. The cat went to find the shaman and ask him for advice.

D

As soon as the Shaman saw the hungry cat, he fed it and listened to its troubles.

"Shaman, no matter how quietly I move, everything sees me coming and runs away! I'm such a poor hunter that I've caught only a few beetles in days! Soon I'll be too weak to catch even those! What shall I do?"

C

"Listen carefully," the shaman told him, "and do just as I say. Go wait in the bushes by the water hole until you see a big bush pig. Then jump out and shout something VERY RUDE!"

B

The yellow cat was puzzled but thanked the shaman for his advice. He hid by the water hole, and soon a huge bush pig came by for a drink. The cat was frightened, but he jumped from his hiding place and shouted, "Ugh! I have never seen such an UGLY beast!"

A

When he awoke, flower-shaped mud spots had dried on his fur. The spots stayed on him forever and made it hard to see him move through the jungle. And that's how the cat we know as ocelot became a good hunter and never went hungry again.

After the pig went away, the cat crawled out of the water. He was too tired even to shake himself off, and fell asleep in the sun.

The angry bush pig whirled around and with a mighty shove, tossed the cat into the muddy water!

Name _____

PAPUA PAINTED FACE

The forest people in New Guinea paint their faces for special occasions. Use crayons or markers to draw your own design on the mask below.

My mask is for _____.

These are some ways they paint their faces.

DISAPPEARING ACT

Rain forests are magnificent but troubled ecosystems. A unit on rain forests wouldn't be complete without mention of the destruction and a thoughtful discussion of possible solutions.

Deforestation of Brazilian Amazon

Paradise Lost

Bulldozed, sawed, and burned, 100 acres of rain forest—about 70 football fields' worth—are being destroyed *every minute*. We've all heard the numbers, but what do they mean? Why are the forests vanishing at such an astounding rate, and what harm will it do?

Who's to Blame?

All of us in developed countries have, as one biologist put it, "our hands on the chain saw." From our mahogany chairs to our appetite for hamburgers, we share responsibility for the destruction of rain forests. While it's easy to point accusing fingers at ranchers, loggers, and farmers, we need to understand the social and economic forces acting on them in order to offer practical solutions.

Economic Impact

Most rain forest countries have weak economies, large national debts, and few resources to create new industries. The developed nations' demand for forest products seems like a quick fix: burn the forest to raise cattle, cut the forest to sell the lumber. Developed nations and multinational banks have often provided huge loans for ill-advised projects, and although a handful have worked, many more have produced only short-term profit and long-term devastation.

> **FOREST FACT**
> In 4 square miles of rain forest there are about 1,500 kinds of flowering plants.

Tropical Woods

In Asia and Africa, logging is big business, and the method of obtaining exotic woods takes its toll on the rain forests. Since individual trees of a species are widely spaced, taking just a few of them can lead to their extinction in a given area. And bringing in heavy equipment to get to those chosen trees causes other damage as well, by mangling roots and gouging trees that happen to be in the way.

The Burger Effect

Our demand for low-cost beef puts pressure on distributors to buy it from Central and South America. To create cattle pastures, huge forest areas are set ablaze. This results in nutrients being released into the soil, producing lush green meadows—for a short while. The cattle-trodden soil quickly erodes, the grassland turns to wasteland, and additional forest must be burned to replace it.

City Farmers

In many countries, the best farming land is outside the forest and is already owned by corporations and wealthy individuals. So when governments "give" forest land to large numbers of poor city people, the offer is rarely refused. Unfortunately, the gifts don't come with instructions on how to farm in a sustainable way. Settlers use the popular slash-and-burn methods to clear the land because that is what everyone else does. Instead of allowing the land to rest and replenish after a few harvests as the indigenous people do, they try to coax more from the thin soil until it's depleted. Then the settlers carve deeper into the forest and continue the destructive process.

What's at Stake?

Since rain forests can't replenish themselves in a few decades—or even a few centuries—there's a terrible finality about burning millions of acres each year.

🌿 The loss of animal and plant species is estimated at *six extinctions every hour.* The wildlife is in the most immediate danger since these animals exist nowhere else.

🌿 Rain forest plants that have already provided so many of our medicines might well be gone before they can be evaluated—and even before we know they exist. Scientists race against deforestation, trying to find cures for heart disease, cancer, AIDS, and other diseases.

🌿 More and more indigenous people are being pushed out of forest areas to make way for new settlers. Their culture is being lost, and the newcomers are exposing them to fatal diseases.

🌿 Rain forest vegetation absorbs carbon dioxide and releases oxygen. The more vegetation there is, the cleaner the air. The widespread burning of forests affects the climate all over the world as carbon dioxide pours into Earth's atmosphere. Many scientists feel strongly that this is a factor in global warming. When there's no vegetation to slow rain, erosive flooding occurs as rivers and streams overflow. On the flip side is drought. Much of the moisture in the air above a rain forest comes from the leaves below when the vegetation "sweats" the water out. But if there's no forest, there's none of this evapotranspiration, and therefore little or no rain.

Finding Solutions

The best way to stop the devastation of rain forests is to offer financial reasons to keep them intact. The two sustainable ways to farm—agroforestry and extractivism—allow products to be harvested without harming the forest. This is how we obtain latex, cashews, palm oil, and medicinal drugs. Using these sustainable farming methods could increase production and substantially raise export revenues. Both wildlife tourism and pharmaceutical exploration could also offer great financial returns for rain forest nations and their people.

SOME GOOD NEWS ABOUT RAIN FORESTS

- During the last 20 years, media coverage of rain forests has been growing, and the consequences of losing such rich ecosystems are sinking in. People around the world are joining programs to help save the rain forests.

- The Rain Forest Action Network mobilized people to boycott a fast food chain that was the largest importer of Central American beef. It took two years, and the persistence of millions of consumers, but eventually the food chain stopped using imported beef.

- Conservation organizations like the World Wildlife Fund and Nature Conservancy are providing funds for rain forest parks and sanctuaries. Environmental associations also work out debt-for-nature deals, in which banks allow rain forest countries to use their debt payments to preserve land.

- International banks are now carefully evaluating the potential environmental impact on rain forests before lending money to less-developed nations for projects.

- The Kuna Indians of Panama are turning 5,000 acres of forest on their reserve into a biological research park.

- The Brazilian rubber tappers have pressured their government to set aside large forest areas just for rubber tapping and the collection of nuts and fruit.

- Huge corporations are trying to improve their ecological images. One multinational firm has funded a Save the Tiger project in Southeast Asia, and another withdrew plans for natural gas exploration in Myanmar and funded a Marine National Park instead.

ACTIVITIES

Rain Forest Report (SCIENCE)

MATERIALS reproducible page 76 ♦ KWL chart ♦ green parrot shapes from Parrot Talk KWL activity on page 11

This activity recaps and assesses what students have learned during their rain forest unit. Copy and distribute page 76. Challenge students to answer as many questions as they can. Then invite them—armed with their reports—to update the classroom's KWL chart. Take answers from them for the **Want to finds out** section and add some of the students' Report facts to the Learned section.

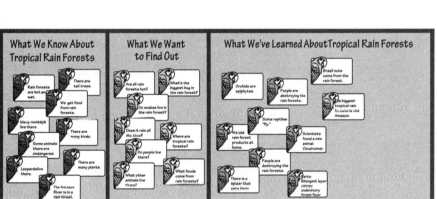

Forest Fund Raising (CROSS-CURRICULAR)

Learning about the problems of the world's rain forests will inspire many students to want to do something to help. There's a list of organizations on page 79 that are working to preserve rain forest ecosystems. Students can contact these for more information on their activities and what your class can do to help. Here are a few ideas for raising money to help fund those efforts.

🍃 The class can hold a tropical bake sale featuring goodies made from bananas, chocolate, coconut, and other rain forest foods. (There's a recipe for a rain forest snack, jungle jumble, on page 75.)

🍃 The class can hold a book drive for the rain forest. Ask parents and PTA members to donate new and used books. When there are enough books, the class can make colorful bookmarks that have rain forest facts on them and hold a book sale. A free bookmark could be included with every purchase.

🍃 A rain forest walkathon can be organized, sponsored by parents and local merchants. Students take money pledges for every mile that they walk. Students could measure the distance they walk in daily amounts of rain forest destroyed or use another significant rain forest statistic.

Culminating Activities (CROSS-CURRICULAR)

As the rain forest unit nears its end, students—either in groups or individually—can demonstrate what they have learned through a culminating activity. The completed projects can be shared and/or displayed during the *moka* celebration. Here are a few ideas.

🍃 **RAIN FOREST TIMES** Student groups can write and publish a newspaper about the rain forest. Articles could cover updates on how different rain forests are faring around the world and what's being done to help. Cartoons, word puzzles, and editorials could also be included.

🍃 **TAKE AN EXPEDITION** Many zoos and natural history museums have rain forest exhibits. If there is one in your area, consider taking your class to visit it.

🍃 **RAIN FOREST DEBATES** What should and could be done about rain forest destruction is a controversial subject and a perfect debate topic. Debate teams can be assigned different sides of rain forest issues.

🍃 **RAIN FOREST ALPHABET** Students can create an alphabet book by drawing a rain forest plant or animal for each letter of the alphabet. The pictures can be collected into a book and displayed on the Discovery Table.

🍃 **RAIN FOREST ANIMAL SPEECH** If the animals of the rain forest could speak, how would they teach people to respect their environment? Have each student write a short speech from a particular rain forest animal's point of view and share it with the class.

🍃 **PICK A RAIN FOREST** Students choose a specific rain forest to research. Then they create a colorful poster that has a map and lists fun facts about that rain forest and its animal and human inhabitants.

🍃 **GROW A RAIN FOREST** Students can grow their own piece of the rain forest in the classroom. Encourage them to bring in avocado pits, orange seeds, or peanuts to grow in the classroom. Students can keep a weekly record of how fast their plant grows and then make a graph of the results comparing growth in these different rain forest plants.

🍃 **RAIN FOREST TRAVEL SHOW** Students can write a script for a TV show that takes its viewers on a tour of the Amazon rain forest. What's it like to meet a harpy eagle or a very large anaconda? What's it like to travel on the Amazon River?

🍃 **RAIN FOREST POLL** Students can design and execute a schoolwide poll on rain forest issues. The results can be graphed and posted in school hallways.

A MERRY MOKA

In Papua New Guinea, a big celebration is called a *moka*. All the relatives and tribal members come together from miles away. There's dancing, chatting, and a lot of food! What better way to celebrate all students have learned about rain forests than by having their own *moka!* Here are some ideas for making it rain forest related.

🍃 **GOODIES!** Your *moka* can feature treats made from rain forest foods like chocolate, coconut, bananas, and rain forest nuts. (There's a recipe for a jungle treat on page 75.) A punch of orange, pineapple, and other rain forest fruit can be served. The table can be decorated with a few live plants or paper bromeliads.

🍃 **GAMES!** Students can play peteca (see page 75), Forest Dominoes (page 36), or What's for Lunch? (page 38).

🍃 **GUESTS!** Invite another class to the *moka* to share in the treats, games, and fun. The guests can tour the Canopy Corner and entertained by a performance of *Too Many Toucans!* (page 35) or a poetry reading (page 77). The class might put together a short informational presentation about the rain forest. Encourage students to share their rain forest projects with their visitors.

🍃 **MUSIC!** Playing tapes of rain forest sounds or music made by rain forest peoples will add atmosphere to your *moka*. Don't forget to play your class Jungle Jamboree tape (page 74).

Jungle Jamboree (MUSIC)

MATERIALS tape recorder ♦ blank audiocassette

The rain forest is a noisy place—birds squawk and chirp, monkeys scream, insects buzz, and rain drips on leaves. Challenge students to re-create some of these sounds and record them. Ask: *What's one sound you might hear in a rain forest?* Write it on the board and ask: *What does that sound like?* Keep listing sounds on the board until you have enough for a class concert (6 to 12). Then have groups of three or four students choose one of the sounds to make. Once students know what sounds they're responsible for, rehearse the jamboree by "conducting" the sound makers like an orchestra—each sound group getting its turn. For the grand finale all the sounds can join in at once. When students have the hang of it, record their jungle jamboree.

The Sloth's Song (LANGUAGE ARTS)

MATERIALS reproducible page 77

The poem on page 77 is about the sluggish sloth of the rain forest. Photocopy and hand out the poem to students. First read the poem aloud, then invite students to read parts of it aloud. And in a final cooperative effort, go around the class giving each student a turn at reading one line (there are 31 lines total).

EXTENSION ACTIVITY Challenge students to create short poems of their own about a rain forest animal of their choice.

TOUCAN
See if you can
Find the toucan
In the leafy tree.

A kinkajou can
Reach the toucan
When it climbs the tree.

Peteca (GAME)

MATERIALS sock ◆ sock stuffing: newspaper, tissue, or Styrofoam pieces ◆ string ◆ four feathers (optional)

Peteca is a Brazilian party game that children play using a smallbean bag or sand-filled sock. As a safe, soft adaptation, fill a sock with very lightweight material, such as crumpled newspaper, Styrofoam peanuts, or facial tissue. Then tie it with a string and attach feathers for decoration.

To play, a group of students try to keep the sock in the air by taking turns hitting it up with one hand (like they would with a balloon). With each successful "hit," that student says a letter of the alphabet or a number. The player to make it through the most letters (or to the highest number) without dropping or missing the sock, wins.

Jungle Jumble (RECIPE)

Here's a yummy treat made from rain forest foods. Substitutions can be made if any items are unavailable, and quantities can be adjusted according to the number of students attending the *moka*.

Place all the ingredients (but don't mix them) in a plastic container with a seal-on lid. Then have students stand in a circle and take turns announcing what they like best about the rain forest before giving the container a shake and passing it on. When everyone has tumbled the container, the jungle jumble should be ready to eat. Students can use small paper cups to scoop out and hold their treats.

JUNGLE JUMBLE

1 cup peanuts
$\frac{1}{2}$ cup Brazil nuts
$\frac{1}{2}$ cup cashew nuts
$\frac{1}{2}$ cup slivered coconut
$\frac{1}{2}$ cup pineapple
$\frac{1}{2}$ cup dried banana chips
$\frac{1}{2}$ cup dried papaya
$\frac{1}{2}$ cup dried mango

Mix all ingredients together in a large plastic container with a seal-on lid. Yields about $4\frac{1}{2}$ cups.

Name _____

RAIN FOREST REPORT

1. An endangered rain forest animal is _____

2. Some foods I like from the rain forest are _____

_____

3. People who live in the rain forest get their food by _____

_____

4. A jungle plant I learned about is _____

5. A neat thing I discovered about the rain forest is _____

_____

_____

6. Rain forests are in trouble because _____

_____

_____

7. Something I will try to do for the rain forest is _____

_____

_____

8. Rain forests are important because _____

_____

_____

THE SLOTH

A living cradle
in my tree,
it's usually snoozle time
for me.
A bag of fur
with hooks for toes,
that's the way
a sloth's life goes.
I nibble on a leaf or two.
It's such slow work
to chew
and chew.
My eyes spy
a slice
of sky.
The wind sings me
a lullaby.
Softly my eyes close
and then
I drift off to sleep
again.
Let the monkeys
leap and run.
My lifestyle's not
for everyone.
I'm not as lazy
as I seem.
I have so many
dreams to dream.
So very many
dreams to dream . . .

—*Bobbi Katz*

Copyright ©1996 by Bobbi Katz

BOOK BREAKS

FOR STUDENTS

At Home in the Rain Forest by Diane Willow (Charlesbridge, 1991)

Enora and the Black Crane by Arone Raymond Meeks (Scholastic, 1993)

Extremely Weird Frogs by Sarah Lovett (John Muir, 1991)

Fernando's Gift by Douglas Keister (Sierra Club, 1995)

The Great Kapok Tree by Lynne Cherry (Gulliver, 1990)

Inside the Amazing Amazon by Don Lessem (Crown, 1995)

Life in the Rain Forests by Lucy Baker (Scholastic, 1990)

Nature's Green Umbrella: Tropical Rain Forests by Gail Gibbons (Morrow, 1994)

Poisoned Paradise (Hardy Boys mystery) by Franklin W. Dixon (Pocket Books, 1993)

Rain Forest by Barbara Taylor (Dorling Kindersley, 1992)

Rain Forest Amerindians by Anna Lewington (Steck-Vaughn, 1993)

Rain Forest Animals by Michael Chinery (Random House, 1992)

Rain Forest Homes by Aklthea Pittaway (Oxford, 1980)

Rain Forest Nature Search (Joshua Morris, 1992)

Tropical Rain Forests by Emilie U. Lepthien (Children's Press, 1993)

Welcome to the Green House by Jane Yolen (Putnam, 1993)

Where the Forest Meets the Sea by Jeannie Baker (Greenwillow Books, 1987)

FOR TEACHERS

The Rain Forests: A Celebration edited by Lisa Silcock (Chronicle Books, 1995)

The Rain Forest by Billy Goodman (Little, Brown, 1991)

Rainforests edited by Norman Myers (Rodale Press, 1993)

ENVIRONMENTAL ORGANIZATIONS

🍃 The Nature Conservancy
1815 North Lynn St.
Arlington, VA 22209

🍃 Wildlife Conservation International
New York Zoological Society
Bronx, NY 10460

🍃 World Wildlife Fund
Conservation Foundation
1250 24th St. NW
Washington, DC 20037

🍃 Rain Forest Action Network
301 Broadway, Suite A
San Francisco, CA 94133

🍃 The Children's Rain Forest
P.O. Box 936
Lewiston, ME 04240

GLOSSARY

algae very simple plants that live in water and damp places

bromeliad tropical plant of the pineapple family that often grows on tree trunks

camouflage color or shape that blends in with the surroundings

canopy the layer of vegetation that forms the "roof" of the rain forest

deforestation the destruction of a forest

emergent a tree that grows higher than the surrounding canopy trees

epiphyte a plant that grows on other plants

indigenous native to, occurring naturally in a specific area

liana a vine rooted in the soil that grows up trees

mammal animal that feeds milk to its young

reptile cold-blooded animal, usually with scales

shaman a tribal healer or priest

species a group of animals or plants that is different from other groups

understory the layer of forest under the canopy

ANIMAL NAME PRONUNCIATION KEY

agouti uh-GOO-tee

anaconda an-nuh-CON-duh

babirusa bab-ih-ROO-suh

coatimundi kuh-wah-ti-MUN-dee

capybara ka-pih-BAR-uh

chameleon kuh-MEEL-yun

cuscus kuss-kuss

fossa FAH-suh

indri IN-dree

kinkajou KIN-kuh-joo

lemur LEE-mur

macaw muh-CAW

okapi oh-KA-pee

pangolin PAN-guh-lin

quetzal KET-sal

tamandua tuh-MAN-doo-uh

tapir TAY-per

tarsier TAR-see-er

tegus TAY-guss

toucan TOO-kahn

urutu uh-ruh-too

ANSWERS

Page 20, Finding Tropical Rain Forests
1. no 2. no 3. South America 4. 5 5. southern 6. west coast 7. Indian Ocean and Pacific Ocean 8. Mexico or Central America 9. Asia 10. Asia **Extra:** a

Page 21, Mapping the Amazon
1. Brazil 2. Atlantic Ocean 3. French Guiana 4. Bolivia 5. Brazil and Peru

Page 39, Rain Forest Riddles
1. sloth 2. tamandua 3. goliath frog 4. parrot snake **Extra:** tamandua and sloth; goliath frog; parrot snake

Page 57, Meet the Cloudrunner
1. mammal 2. fruits, nuts, and insects 3. runs around the misty treetops 4. Night; it has large eyes to see in the dark. 5. squirrel, potto, kinkajou, etc. **Extra:** remote area, not very many of them, out at night